Silvery Gleanings

Poems by
Delores T. Taylor

Omaha, Nebraska

©2020 Delores T. Taylor

All rights reserved. No part of this publication may be reproduced in any form for any purpose without the express written permission of the publisher.

Published by
SpirWrit Publishing, Omaha, Nebraska
SpirWrit@conciergemarketing.com
Paperback ISBN: 978-1-7344061-4-6
Mobi ISBN:978-1-7344061-5-3
Library of Congress Cataloging Number: 2020904024

PRINTED IN THE UNITED STATES OF AMERICA
10 9 8 7 6 5 4 3 2 1

This book of poetry is dedicated to those who like a good poem as well as a good cup of hot coffee.

Contents

INTRODUCTION 1	SNOWCAPPED SPRUCE 53
IMAGES OF SORROW 3	MY NEMESIS 55
NEIGHBORLY BLUES 5	ORACLE 57
CREAMED RIVALRY 7	CROWDS 59
LAYERS 9	PAINT 61
OCEAN FLOOR 11	BULLY 63
SMASHING AVOCADOS 13	LOTTERY WINNER 65
MUD PIES 15	HAYRIDE 67
WHISPERING PINES 17	ANCESTRY 69
SITTING ON A PARK BENCH ... 19	LONG WAY HOME 71
CLEAN BREAK 21	LOCAL PARADE 73
SIMPLY LIVING 23	LIGHTHOUSE 75
DO IT 25	BEAUTY UNMASKED 77
I WANT TO KNOW YOU BETTER 27	LOSER BLUES 79
THE STRANGER 29	LOST SUITCASE 81
STOREHOUSE 31	GRATITUDE ON DISPLAY 83
HOLIDAY RECKONING 33	PORCH GOSSIP 85
CABIN SONG 35	HAMMOCK RESPITE 87
SPIDER BLUE 37	FIREWORKS 89
WIDOW'S PEAK 39	RIP CORD 91
WHO WILL? 41	CHANDELIER MAGIC 93
SUNSHINE 43	ANTHILL 95
BIRD ALERT 45	THIRTY 97
GOODWILL FINDS 47	GRANDKIDS 99
SIDEWALK FLOWER 49	SEVENTY 103
THE DIRGE 51	ACKNOWLEDGMENTS 105
	ABOUT THE AUTHOR 107

Hello! Let SILVERY GLEANINGS entertain you a bit
I hope you'll find each poem a hit,
Perhaps, you'll even want to share this book
With those who want to take a look.

Enjoy the freshness and the wit
As you stand or sit,
It might trigger a myriad of reactions
But all to your satisfaction.

I had fun working with each title
Forming its existence as one preparing for a recital,
Life has an uncanny way of sprouting food for thought
Making one conscious of what is being taught.

Sorrow is a bitter sandwich that requires intermittent chewing.

Images of Sorrow

Sorrow lurks behind every winding path
Stretching forth its icy hands
Engulfing the spidery sighs of happiness
Bleaching ebony flesh to a whitewashed knoll

Sorrow raises its lofty head
Looming with malignant and rancid overtures
Depleting the vibrant vigil
Scoffing the distraught and leashing dreams

An arc of purple, brown, and gray
Embezzler of the green, yellow, and red.

Strong drink plays the fool to forced happiness.

Neighborly Blues

Greetings, my fellow neighbor,
(Oh yes, it is Saturday night!)
There he goes lurching and cavorting
Heralding the times.

The lithe figure flaunts his jaunty being
With loquacious gibberish
That only he dare decipher.

His camaraderie is with the generous
Libation that diffuses in his body like the spokes on a wheel
Yielding slurred speech and limpid eyes.

Weaving in and out of traffic
As a lax cast away
Castrated by years of predestined toil.

He beseechingly moans
Unraveling hurt, joy, pain, and pleasure
Awakening his unkempt load
To the tune of a mesmerizing blues.

An opponent is the tinder in your soul that ignites you into victory.

Creamed Rivalry

Meshed in a vintage potpourri of novelty the two sat stone-faced and lucid
Amid the fumes of condemnation whirling messages of fright

One emerges and gleams the tide of anticipation
That haunts the still night

The other locks his shoulders and embraces rage
Stretching toward a new height

The path is entwined and a bemuddled sight
Blinded by fate and fury the rage forms a new light
Fused with determination and selfish might
The fight starts and there is no winner tonight

Realization formed a glazed medley of hot delight
Simmering in a potion of deceit and conformity
Highlighted by the need to consider hindsight

There is no winner where bad meets bad
Only a unified cup of venom nursed by fad
Ultimately, they know the union is too sad

Dreams wasted – dreams destroyed – dreams creamed

$\mathcal{L}$ove is a bedspread for discolored, ripped, and unguarded sheets.

Layers

Peel back my blanket of rue
Flip through each fleshly disk;
Take out one and play it through
Enter my heart at your own risk.

Sift through each slice of woe
Rearrange all the fragmented pain;
Pick another disk and rub away the sticky foe
Fold it gently and keep it from the rain.

As you lift the last fragile piece
Crumbled against a bed of crimson hurt;
Mold it gently and press a new crease
Bury it in a new cavern covered in dirt.

Why did it take so long to fix me?
Pour your balm of comfort in each cell;
Let your love set me free
Garner the calloused pieces, and don't let us fail.

Freshen me with your cooling mist
Hold me close and savor each beat;
Shelter me from harm as you lock your wrist
How wonderful it is that we got to meet.

When life throws you to the bottom, sit upright until you can float to the top.

Ocean Floor

Looking up, looking around, looking down
I keep on thinking about my life,
Because what goes around comes around
Where pain pierces me like a knife.

Take me to the ocean floor
Beauty lies deep within unseen;
Let me see the beauty in store,
Colors sparkling and glimmering unto a queen.

I can't stop to look deep down,
For I have to watch the eagle soar;
Otherwise, you'll see me frown
Take me down slowly to the ocean floor.

Do the fish look up and say –
I'm going to leave this floor and rise?
There's got to be a better day;
Give me a moment to shed this guise.

Ocean floor
      Down no more,
I've got to climb higher
      Higher, powerful, I'm a flier;
I'm reaching, reaching, reaching for the sky
Bye, Bye, Ocean Floor,
Ocean Floor, bye, bye.

*F*ind an unconventional way to thwart the deluge of hurt and pain.

Smashing Avocados

You called me today to say
You've been thinking about our groove,
There's got to be a better way
So you think you'll make a move.

Well, I was about to fix a fabulous avocado meal
But you're not worthy of the way I feel.
Then you went ahead and broke our deal,
And I'm left confused, irritated, for real.

Avocados on the countertop
Somehow fell onto the floor;
I'm doing a crazy hop
As I smash all six and more.

So you want to call it quits,
Smash my love into tiny bits;
I'll make a call to you tomorrow
To tell you that there's no sorrow.

Smashing avocados
Until I feel the pit buried under my feet;
Until all the green oozes free to a different beat,
Until my anger no longer recognizes its meat.

When a confidant betrays, forgive, and let karma ensue.

Mud Pies

She was my childhood friend
I claimed her as next of kin;
We went everywhere, as a mighty duo
"I got your back," was a trusting echo.

But when we got older, we drifted apart
At first it left a pain in my heart;
Until I found out she was dating my ex
I hated her, and my spirit she did vex.

How could she do such a thing
We celebrated when he gave me a ring;
Now she acts like she doesn't care
When we accidentally meet, she holds a stare.

She'll get it back one day
I've moved on, and I have nothing more to say;
I suppose mud will always be a mess
A sloppy, dirty, counterfeit would be my guess.

He broke her heart and left her on a farm
She lost her house, but I wish her no harm;
This is now a very sloppy mud pie
It's just dessert in anybody's eye.

Nature provides solace to forlornness.

Whispering Pines

I hear the wind's shrill voice
Gathering speed faster than my Rolls Royce
It gyrates through each relenting pine
Playing melodies so mysterious, yet free.

What musical language is this I hear?
Sweeping up and down each wooden peer
I stopped to capture its full note
And linger a while and wantonly dote.

Confident and tall
A beacon to the small
Answering nature's call
Through its intricately woven pine wall.

Here, I cherish the sound
As it swirls all around
Its depth or height is not bound
What a marvelous choir I've found.

𝒰nbridled aloneness is the creepage that corrodes the heart.

Sitting On A Park Bench

I sit
 alone thoughtful lazily dreamily agitated longingly

I watch
 boats passing by people walking dogs kids swinging

I hear
 birds chirping waves crashing horns blowing

I taste
 sadness rejection reality

I wait
 hoping someone will share my bench pretending to read

I leave
 alone vexed empty blaming changed

A gut reaction is a stopwatch to denote change.

Clean Break

Heartache and despair caused me to doubt
That somewhere I turned onto the wrong route;
I don't want to experience that lonely road again
Hugged up with Ruby Sue, my friend.

Well, as I continued down the road as fast as I could
I caught a glimpse of a red cardinal above my hood;
No cares for him, not even a wicked thought
Life chooses to shelter and protect what it sought.

Just like the cardinal, an angel did appear
He gazed at me as if my body was clear;
He said, "There's trouble down the road – turn around."
I made a clean break and said, "Thanks," without a sound.

My life was turned around and spared
I said goodbye to misery now that someone cared;
Now my days are filled with hope
Maneuvering my way swinging on life's mercy rope.

Take the time to appraise yourself, and your way of doing things.

Simply Living

Take a closer look at my rose
That takes you into an upright pose;
The smell which lingers into thin air
Then leaves you feeling less than fair.

Take a taste of life's vineyard within reason
Slowly basking in its juices for a season;
Time and time again life's lessons recur,
Making your head swim into a blur.

Take a gentler feel of life's patterns
Folding and tucking each memory under lanterns;
Hearing the voices of "You must" and "You have to"
Swallowing the depths of your dreams in powder blue.

I'm simply living for today
Pushing the past far away
Taking it one leaf at a time,
Some thoughts are not worth a dime.

𝒫rocrastination is the saboteur of furtherance.

Do It

I want to do this
I want to do that
I want to visit my sis
I want to wear a new hat

I want to sing here
I want to sing there
I want to sing to masses
I want to take classes

I'm going to do it
Watch me unfold like a spring lily;
Here I go, making a hit,
Drowning all doubt, seemingly silly.

Yea, I'm doing it better than ever
I'm doing it clever,
I've got to do me
I've got to be free.

Vulnerability is a cracked egg that gently oozes its core.

I Want to Know You Better

Where is the real you?
Is it hiding among the thorns of life
Barely peeking out for sunshine and warmth
Crouching lower in the throes of uncertainty.

What has veiled you?
Open the portals of your heart and let me in
Consider my love as your lifeline
As you dig into your cloistered basin of doubt.

Come away and bare your scars
Allow the salve of sympathy to soothe you
No judgment will spew from my lips
Tell me what makes you recoil and strike.

You are not alone in your pain
Let go and cuddle with truth and trust
You're not that different from most
We all have experiences that warp our vision.

What will it take to pry your heart open?
Let me in
Dump your fears
Open the prison door.

Complexities of a new city, new surroundings, and city people can likely bombard a rural person's footing, dialect, and self-esteem.

The Stranger

Do you know me?
A deserter of a small town desiring to see new land
Left behind only teardrops on the speckled sand.

In the new city my eyes were opened to newer situations
Newer meanings of the word "live"
Strange stares and unwelcomed sighs were what most give.

They attempted to rebuild my body, reconstruct my mind,
Alter my language, and rehabilitate my style
Leaving me as a depressed mold of regenerated bile.

Rebellion entered
I resented change
A country girl well out of her range.

Touch me not
Inconsiderate, blind society
Let me remain me.

The song of my life is imprinted in the sand
A green, black, and red sepulchral mound
Enclosed with an ancestral band.

𝓐 metal house of information, a computer is not greater than its programmer.

Storehouse

Why sit you still and dare to contradict?
Your belly bulges with anticipation
I hear the click of your concentration
As you devour words, symbols, and logic.

Is life the memory void of emotions?
Your brain thrives on electricity and feeds on another's intellect
Selfishness rules your crude devotion,
Yet, you seek the command of a fleshly hand.

I visit you daily and play taps on your frame
You accept my meat and perform your task,
I dare to ask your name
Metal, wires, and plastics form your mask.

Your reputation remains anew
I'm hidden from the world's view;
They seek your knowledge, fun, and games
My reputation remains the same.

Your immortal body rejects time
Unlike this mortal body of mine,
A technician is your only risk
Medicine and physician I can't resist.

Family gatherings trigger moments of fun and craziness

Holiday Reckoning

Festive uniting call –
    hugging
    kissing
    laughing

    barbequing
    grilling
    baking

    singing
    dancing
    drinking

    joking
    lying
    arguing

    gaming
    relaxing
    photographing

Cherished places may keep you vacillating between the desire to maintain or to release.

Cabin Song

I'm missing you today
Longing for your two-room embrace
In your dusty ligneous lair
Where I don't have a care

Standing noonday without my reps
Waiting to climb your wobbly steps
Pressing through the rotten door
Hearing the creaking of your floor

Looking dimly through the dingy windowpane
Where the only washing is from the rain
I imagine my stay to be serene
Just as the sleeping toy soldiers in the vitrine

I'm contemplating whether to sell
The one true heart in this vale
Will another appreciate your style
Snuggled in front of a ravine and a woodpile

𝓛oyal pets give a surmountable expanse of friendship and adoration.

Spider Blue

Spider Blue
Ever so true
I am stuck on you
Loving you through and through
You protect me
You love me
We enjoy walks in the park
As you extend your rhythmic bark
Through rain and snow
I take the leash and off we go
You pummel the sidewalk through the wind
My loving, loyal, furry friend
A sophisticated catch
We are a good match
Let's get a snack
And head on back
You gently and persistently woo
My adorable Spider Blue

Distinguishing traits carve out an arc of pedigree.

Widow's Peak

Sculptured
Like a river's edge
You wear a
Designer's tag
That makes its mark
Vividly to a point
Upon the forehead
What a crafty design
Symmetrical to the nose
Instructed hair
Knows boundaries
Ready to stop
Ponder
Redirect
Pretty cool artistry
Well-etched formation
A beautician's masterpiece.

Antithetical thoughts mirror sadness and joy.

Who Will?

Who will cheer for me
When I run a marathon
    Who will mourn for me
    When I lose my health
Who will cheer for me
When I graduate from college
    Who will mourn for me
    When I can't find a job
Who will cheer for me
When I marry
    Who will mourn for me
    When I get divorced
Who will cheer for me
When I make my first million
    Who will mourn for me
    When I am bankrupt
Who will cheer for me
When I retire
    Who will mourn for me
    When I die

Partaking of what's both beneficial and harmful demands scrutiny.

Sunshine

Medicinal rays
    Drop down Vitamin D
    From you it's totally free

Blinding rays
    Shift the clouds to block your glare
    So I can comfortably stare

Soothing rays
    Bathe me with your warm embrace
    Dissolve the wrinkles aiming to deface

Piercing rays
    Tan me a golden brown
    So I'll be the talk of the town

Escapism frees the soul,
but confines the body.

Bird Alert

When you fly south today
Allow me to soar with you
So free, fearless, and focused
Making your way across the sky.

I won't be a problem
I trust your navigation
Who am I to dictate your direction
Or interrupt your schedule.

I am welcomed into the fleet
I'm in awe, each a team player
Nameless and voiceless I glide
Mission driven, electing to please.

I'm tired and cold; I asked to go home
They speak, but I am ignorant
We shifted direction and flew down
My friends tweeted and militarily exited.

Buying resale is a way to save money while enjoying the hunt.

Goodwill Finds

I frequently shop a Goodwill store
It is never a bore
I browse and critique
As if I'm in a boutique

An item usually catches my eye
So I'll tuck it in the cart to buy
Then I'll approach the next aisle
Adding to my discriminate pile

    Bargain scavenger
    Jewelry connoisseur
    Garment label huntress
    Book explorer

I found deals galore
With prices I couldn't ignore
Until next time
I'll save each found dime

𝓢trength manifests itself through different sizes, shapes, and formations.

Sidewalk Flower

I salute your tenacity
Your grand determination
To squeeze through the concrete
Like a newborn baby

I searched for bruises
I found none
Here it stands so stately and prim
Wearing only a smirk

I want to pluck it
Each day I refuse
It deserves to live
Such a fighter, I see

𝒟eath leaves a void
that is only filled by
shatterproof memories.

The Dirge

You left too soon
Death is stealthy and deep
Couldn't wait until noon
Died last night in your sleep

I hope you had a swell life
Much pomp and circumstance at the egress
Mourners are pained as if by a knife
I trust you lived without regret

Did you have an escort during ascent,
Or a friendly cohort as guide?
Did you see and smell the hyacinth,
Was your journey far and wide?

I'm missing you a heap
We'll met again I know
But now the hurt is deep
As I'm on earth below.

𝒩ature's beauty, endorsed by snow, is captivating, fanciful, and fleeting.

Snowcapped Spruce

As I gaze at my tree
What a wonder do I see
A hat wearing greenery
To boost the wintry scenery

In December it's dressed in colored lights
That lift my mood on blustery nights
Kids say my tree affords them much joy
Better than any outdoor toy

The icy hat is not yours to keep
Into your eyelids it will seep
Finishing the melt in the sun
And down your cheeks it will run

Advice can be bittersweet, and it can even backfire.

My Nemesis

He makes me laugh heartily
    I'm sad when he leaves
He dares me to eat exotic foods
    I vomit
He challenges me at chess
    I lose money
He introduces me to cute guys
    I unfriend them on Facebook
He shows me magic tricks
    I feel gullible
He suggests I try new things
    I wet my pants sky diving
He persuades me to buy designer clothes
    I go to thrift stores
He encourages me to exercise
    I walk to the mailbox
He advises me to get a makeover
    I dyed my hair orange.

A whistling teakettle reaches its potential with a cryptic sound.

Oracle

Sage
Scatter your thoughts
Slather them among hearers

Drown skepticism
Delegate followers
Douse hope

Warn of the epidemic
Wake stagnant dreams
Win

Ease tensions
Elevate spirits
Embellish truth

Being lost in artificial comradery converging on purposeful agenda can be endearing.

Crowds

I like to submerge within a crowd
My aloneness ceases to be
It has a vibe of its own
Moving to some unheard ditty

It houses a streak of pleasure
Though short-lived
As destination imposes
The crowd disperses

A favorite is a football crowd
It's pumped and ready to go
Screams and chants hover
Like dew on morning grass

I feel as though I belong
To this vessel pulsating strong
I want to say goodbye
But no one is aware of me

Spruce it up a bit with color.

Paint

On walls
    invigorating
    refreshing
    perky
    rejuvenating
On houses
    vibrant
    tempered
    emulsive
    flashy
On cars
    sleek
    shiny
    bold
    beautiful
On art
    vertical
    horizontal
    streaky
    splotchy

A bully is a bag
of wind that loses its
direction, leaves venom
along the way, and needs
a harness and a rebuke.

Bully

A bully enrolled at my school
He chose to be a fool,
One day he snatched my lunch
I lost control and threw a punch.

He called me a bad name
And said my mother was the same,
I swallowed hard and curled my fist
For he was on my "gitcha" list.

I walked toward home and so did he
Maybe now he'll let me be,
I felt a rock hit my neck
I quickly ran onto my deck.

I told my dad what he did
He said, "That's a bad kid."
We reported him to the principal
To prove to him he's not invincible.

*M*oney is an individual's servant, and not a person's master.

Lottery Winner

Our neighbor was a winner
He invited us over for dinner
We thought he would change
And think himself out of our range

He remained modest and nice
Lottery playing is like throwing dice
He gave my family a lavish trip
Showing that money had no ghastly grip

We watched him over the years
Let go of his monetary fears
He kept his job as a cook
And put his recipes in a book

He bought his mother a new home and car
By doing that he really raised the bar
He bought himself a boat
And gave his wife a fur coat

*J*ovial experiences that make you act as a kid again is like buried treasure.

Hayride

The ride makes me giddy
A pleasant change from the city
It's lofty and bumpy
Quaint and lumpy

A quartet is seated below
Singing merrily and all aglow
The air is damp
At this old camp

Round and round
Uphill and down
The wagon careens
Dips and leans

The ride comes to a halt
We are all given a chocolate malt
There's hot apple cider
Enough for each lively rider

Keys that unlock who you are tend to be found among ancestral doors.

Ancestry

Blood linked
Forever tied
Kindred spirits
Love

Fears
Struggles
Dreams
Triumphs

Waymakers
Torchbearers
Supporters
Changers

Strength
Perseverance
Courage
Pride

To some, going home is where you feel akin to surroundings and like a magnet to family.

Long Way Home

Nestled in the driver's seat
With the heat on my feet,
I engulf the sights
Heading for Cedar Heights.

Here's the four-way stop
A laundromat I used to mop,
The gas station that sold good wings
The pizza parlor where I'd take my flings.

The theatre sign is rusted
Windowpanes are busted,
Oh, there's Pete with his dog
Walking in the fog.

Down the graveled road I go
Where tree limbs hang low,
The roadside deer gave me a fright
Slowly, I turned to my house on the right.

Garnering a slice of mobile pleasure via a parade frees youthful energy.

Local Parade

Got my chair planted on the edge
The crowd so thick, cramped in a wedge,
Eagerly, I chew my gum
Hearing music in my head, I begin to hum.

As the parade begins, I see the marching bands
I tap the beat with imaginary sticks in my hands,
Appearing are the breathtaking vintage cars
Following are motorcycles with shiny handlebars.

Drooling fans gaze at firetrucks and floats
Kids reach high for candy to stuff in totes,
Thrown by clowns and businesspeople too
Balloons break free as if by cue.

Drill teams are fun to watch
In unison, they take the dance up a notch,
Police ride at the very end
Signaling the parade is over at the bend.

Loss grips and freezes
the heart for a set time,
then it loosens its grip to
release life to begin again.

Lighthouse

This lighthouse
Is a beacon for my ship
A beacon for me
To try new adventures
Off the sea
Lighthearted and inquisitive
I need to shed light
On a subject of reclusion
The man I loved drowned
His body was never recovered
I married the ominous sea
Sailed alone for ten years
Now I'm ready for onshore love
        Pure
        True
Unmeasured by a plumb line

Be true to yourself, and embrace your beauty and uniqueness.

Beauty Unmasked

Kinky hair
Big nose
Thick lips
Wide hips
Bow legs

LOVELY   BEAUTIFUL   PROUD

Promulgating:
                        Sensitivity
                        Humor
                        Profundity
                        Generosity
                        Grandiosity

Accept a challenge, do your best, and know that your best is enough.

Loser Blues

Don't be sad
It's not that bad
Someone had to win
Losing is not a sin

You played long and hard
You didn't let down your guard
There's always another chance
To execute your victory dance

Chin up
Raise the cup
Shoulders back
You're the head of the pack

Don't think about the score
Give the fans autographs once more
Grin and bear the lost
Get back out there at any cost

When you lose that
special something,
though it may be painful,
be assured that material
things can be replaced.

Lost Suitcase

I took a trip
Arrived home
My suitcase did not
Where could it be?
Is it lonely for me?

Here's the key
To fit the lock
Of my favorite suitcase
Return to me
You carry my new lingerie

Under my four dresses
Are necklaces and earrings
At the bottom are expensive shoes
In the zippered bag is eight hundred dollars
Break loose
Return to me

Giving with a sincere
heart is a
two-sided hoist.

Gratitude On Display

A quick visit to a restaurant
changed my life,
The host seated me.
A waitress came to my table and
introduced herself sobbing and
wiping away tears.
I said, "What's wrong?"
She said, "I'm a mother of three and
yesterday I lost everything in a house fire."
I sat numbed.
I thanked her for coming to work,
despite the loss,
She told me that she needed the money.
I was given excellent service;
I thanked her for taking good care of me.
She filled my water glass,
and gave me the bill;
I took out my checkbook,
and wrote out a check to her
for five thousand dollars.
As I was leaving,
I saw her head to my table;
Then I heard a piercing scream.
I said to myself, "She got it!"

Gossip is a knife with a crooked and dull blade.

Porch Gossip

At dusk
I saw four hens
Seated on a porch
They huddled and cackled
Juicy gossip spewed
They clapped their thighs
Threw back their heads
And let loose
A deafening guffaw
Gusto reactivated
Nuggets of gossip
Pecked to shreds
Until there was nothing new to tell

Delight yourself in the freedom to be pampered and genuinely relaxed.

Hammock Respite

Lazily sprawled in summer bliss
My hammock retreat I won't miss,
I'm unhinged and free
With positive thoughts offering glee.

Peace and well-deserved rest
Lounging is what I do best,
No phone calls to interrupt
Until it's time to sup.

Hypnotic sounds lull me to sleep
Releasing stress bottled so deep,
My masseuse is the gentle breeze
With sprinkles that I graciously seize.

It's time to climb out of my den
Amasser of solitude is a sure win,
I saunter through my empty hall
Observing nostalgic pictures hanging on the wall.

Celebrating with fireworks seals anticipation with exhilaration.

Fireworks

Celebration fire
Flung high in the sky
Releasing color bursts
With a bang
A masterful décor of
Eye candy
Shapes and sounds
Rallying for attention
Pop, Pop, Pop
Swish, Swish, Swish
Bang, Bang, Bang
Stay up there
Don't fall down
I need more time
To digest your beauty

Daring and danger are poor players to common sense and forbearance.

Rip Cord

Frozen with fear
I am going to jump
I'm trusting my landing gear
As my heart gives a thump

Suppose my parachute doesn't open!

Should I change my mind?

I'm not that brave
I value my life
Forget all the rave
I'm a pilot's wife

Another took her turn
The rip cord failed
We watched with utmost concern
Unto her death she wailed

Exquisite lighting strikes a pose and parallels to fine dining and runway clothes.

Chandelier Magic

Sparkling and regal
The chandelier commands attention
All eyes on its massive base
Dripping with brilliance

At every angle
It radiates energy and splendor
Iridescent
Intricately glowing

Fixation
Fascination

If I turn my gaze
I'll miss its flirting movement
A reflection caught
A wink

Small wonders and grand creations hold us spellbound and speechless.

Anthill

With untiring efforts to build your hill
You work steadily to make the fill
A collectivized craft
A methodical graft

You are as busy as a bee
Scrambling on bended knee
What fancy footwork at hand
To make a splendor in the sand

What a work of art!
I should put it on a cart
Out of harm's way
To preserve it for a day

Not looking where he was walking
But focused on intense talking
A size eleven shoe crushed the anthill
For all their sweat and toil, they deserve a dollar bill

Living purposely is not a stride, but a punt.

Thirty

3 and 0 came and went
It came in like a flash
Thirty yellow flowers sent
I had a thirties' day bash.

I can't say I feel any different though
There are dreams to catch, and dreams to let go
Resolutions to scratch, and some to keep low
Why age makes a difference, I really don't know.

Journaling has become very dear
I can write nasty notes without any fear
Regrets are few, and good times are near
Now that thirty is not ahead, but in the rear.

Who cares about a number, whether young or old
Attack each year being confident and bold
Age has no sting, or even a solid hold
It does add maturity and wisdom, so I'm told.

So come yearly with your addition
I welcome you, and then dismiss you
Challenges and goals complement fruition
I know who I am and that remains true.

Grandkids are the wealth that keeps on giving.

Grandkids

Grandkids are wonderful and grand
They stretch your bragging rights like a rubber band;
How soon they fall for electronic gadgets
And find their way in the local pageants.

You'll want to shield them from all hurt
And spare them of wallowing in the dirt;
They'll grow so fast, and their appearance will change
Their sizes will fluctuate, and interests will run the range.

You'll have a remedy for each scrape or bruise
Digital photographs and videos of every cruise;
Their names will be on your Facebook page
Along with a series of special events and even their age.

When they come to visit, you will want them to stay
You'll pull out the games and cards for them to play;
Their favorite foods will be on the stove
Cakes, pies, cookies, and candy in the pantry cove.

They will ask you why your hair is gray
And why you do things your particular way;
They will question the whereabouts of your missing tooth
Even gaze at those wrinkles that stole your youth.

How precious they are!
You'll want to preserve each moment in your memory jar;
A bit of you will always be in them
You'll recognize it still as your eyesight grows dim.

What wisdom can you impart to them?
What legacy can you leave for them?
Your love for them will grow stronger each day
They will remember the fun things you had to say.

Age ripens the
retina of wisdom.

Seventy

My rugged friend comes with a counter in hand
He leaves another gem like a faithful fan,
Then strolls stealthily away as only he can
No harp-filled melodies accompany his one man band.

Threescore and ten I've been here
The elements have tarnished my gear,
But there is one thing perfectly clear
If you keep breathing, you'll gain another year.

I'm not sure how to feel about this age
Hopefully, I'll continue to be a sage,
I've completed hundreds of Word Finds and the Maze
No real retirement or laziness, for I'm quite ablaze.

Some friends have moved to a higher place
They've weathered the storms to finish their race,
But sufficient to us all is His grace
Until we behold Him face to face.

Life gives you a manuscript daily. Read it. Prepare your tomorrow with additions and deletions.

Enjoy Life!

Acknowledgments

I would like to thank Amber, my daughter, for believing in me and giving me that extra push to make this book of poems come to fruition. She has been the driving force that allows me to hone my craft and share my creativity.

In addition, my brother, Allen, is very supportive of my writings, and is eager for me to publish more books.

Also by Delores T. Taylor

Available at SpirWrit.com, Amazon.com

About the Author

The author, Delores T. Taylor, was a high school teacher for thirty-seven years. She taught in Virginia and Nebraska. She was born and reared in Virginia, but has been a resident of Nebraska for four decades. She is the mother of two, Keiron and Amber; grandmother of two, Xavier and Halle. The author enjoys writing in different genres, and has published two poetry books. She now spends her time traveling, reading, writing, teaching, and being a chaplain.

Alphabetical Listing of Poems

Ancestry 69	Lost Suitcase 81
Anthill 95	Lottery Winner 65
Beauty Unmasked 77	Mud Pies 15
Bird Alert 45	My Nemesis 55
Bully 63	Neighborly Blues 5
Cabin Song 35	Ocean Floor 11
Chandelier Magic 93	Oracle 57
Clean Break 21	Paint 61
Creamed Rivalry 7	Porch Gossip 85
Crowds 59	Rip Cord 91
Do It 25	Seventy 103
Fireworks 89	Sidewalk Flower 49
Goodwill Finds 47	Simply Living 23
Grandkids 99	Sitting On A Park Bench 19
Gratitude On Display 83	Smashing Avocados 13
Hammock Respite 87	Snowcapped Spruce 53
Hayride 67	Spider Blue 37
Holiday Reckoning 33	Storehouse 31
I Want To Know You Better 27	Sunshine 43
Images Of Sorrow 3	The Dirge 51
Layers 9	The Stranger 29
Lighthouse 75	Thirty 97
Local Parade 73	Whispering Pines 17
Long Way Home 71	Widow's Peak 39
Loser Blues 79	Who Will? 41

www.ingramcontent.com/pod-product-compliance
Lightning Source LLC
Chambersburg PA
CBHW032006080426
42735CB00007B/525